Anonymous

A short account of Algiers

Containing a description of the climate of that country, of the manners and

customs of the inhabitants

Anonymous

A short account of Algiers
Containing a description of the climate of that country, of the manners and customs of the inhabitants

ISBN/EAN: 9783743368743

Manufactured in Europe, USA, Canada, Australia, Japa

Cover: Foto ©Andreas Hilbeck / pixelio.de

Manufactured and distributed by brebook publishing software
(www.brebook.com)

Anonymous

A short account of Algiers

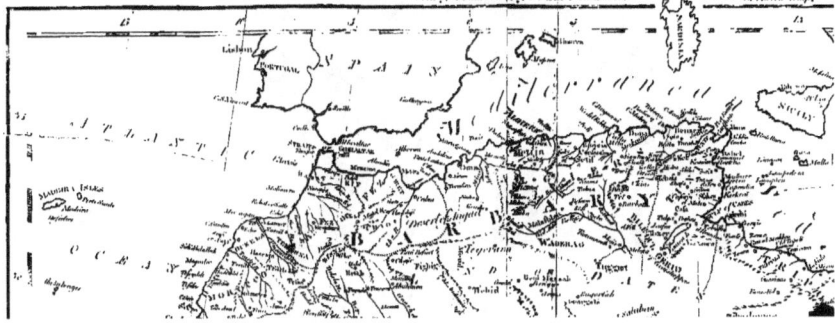

sold by Mathew Carey . N.118 . Market street

A
SHORT ACCOUNT

OF

ALGIERS.

CONTAINING

A DESCRIPTION

OF THE

CLIMATE OF THAT COUNTRY,

OF THE

MANNERS AND CUSTOMS

OF THE

INHABITANTS,

AND OF THEIR SEVERAL WARS AGAINST SPAIN, FRANCE, ENGLAND, HOLLAND, VENICE, AND OTHER POWERS OF EUROPE, FROM THE USURPATION OF *BARBAROSSA* AND THE INVASION OF THE EMPEROR *CHARLES V.* TO THE PRESENT TIME;

WITH A CONCISE

VIEW OF THE ORIGIN

OF THE RUPTURE

BETWEEN

ALGIERS AND THE UNITEDSTATES.

Aut bifce tellus in patulos fpecus,
Ætherve flammis perde fequacibus
Turpes colonos, AFRICANÆ
Dedecus, opprobriumque terræ.

BUCHANAN.

PHILADELPHIA:
Printed by J. Parker for M. Carey, No. 118, Market-ſtreet;
January 8, 1794.

Diſtrict of Pennſylvania, to wit—

(L. S.) BE it remembered, that on the eighth day of January, in the eighteenth year of the independence of the united ſtates of America, Mathew Carey, of the ſaid diſtrict, hath depoſited in this office, the title of a book, the right whereof he claims as proprietor, in the words following, to wit :

" A ſhort account of Algiers, containing a deſcription of
" the climate of that country, of the manners and cuſtoms
" of the inhabitants, and of their ſeveral wars againſt
" Spain, France, England, Holland, Venice and other pow-
" ers of Europe, from the uſurpation of Barbaroſſa and the
" invaſion of the emperor Charles V. to the preſent time,
" with a conciſe view of the origin of the rupture between
" Algiers and the united ſtates." In conformity to the act
of the congreſs of the united ſtates, intituled, " An act for
" the encouragement of learning ; by ſecuring the copies of
" maps, charts, and books, to the authors and proprietors of
" ſuch copies, during the time therein mentioned."

SAMUEL CALDWELL, Clerk of
the diſtrict of Pennſylvania.

SHORT ACCOUNT, &c.

CHAP. I.

General description of the country of Algiers. Clima. Sea-Coast. Principal cities.

ALGIERS is a country, which derives its name from its metropolis ; and extends four hundred and eighty miles in length from east to west along the northern coast of Africa. Its utmost breadth is three hundred and twenty miles, but at the distance of an hundred miles from the sea-coast, that part of Africa becomes a barren desert, almost utterly uninhabitable either by man or beast. Algiers is situated between thirty-two and thirty-seven degrees of north latitude, which corresponds to that of the United States, from Virginia to Carolina, inclusive. It is bounded on the north by the Mediterranean sea ; on the south, by mount Atlas ; on the east, by the country of Tunis ; and on the west, by the river Mulvia, which separates it from the empire of Morocco.

The principal rivers, which water the territory of Algiers, rise in Mount Atlas, and run by a northerly direction into the Mediterranean sea. They are seven in number. None of them has a long course, or even is navigable ; at least none of them is made use of in navigation. It is however likely that they might be employed for this purpose, were the inhabitants of a more intelligent and industrious character ; for some of them are of a tolerable depth. Such is the gross ignorance of the natives in whatever concerns domestic improvement, that there is not a single bridge over any of these rivers. When they are to be crossed, the traveller hath sometimes to wander for several miles in search of a ford, as ferry-boats are unknown. If a heavy rain happens to fall, he is forced to wait, till the river returns to its usual size.

This country confifts of eighteen provinces. The climate is remarkably delightful. The air is pure and ferene. The foil is covered with almoft a perpetual verdure. Extreme heat is not common. This defcription applies to the lands on the fea-coaft; for as we advance into the country, the foil becomes more parched and barren. Indeed a confiderable part of the back country is a favage defert, abounding with lions, tigers, leopards, buffaloes, wild boars, and porcupines. And it muft be acknowledged, that thefe animals are not the leaft amiable inhabitants of this country.

There are few towns of any confequence, though when fucceffively under the dominion of Carthage and Rome, it abounded with populous cities. Bona is fuppofed to be the fame place with the ancient Hippo, a fea-port built by the ancients. It was formerly the capital of the province of Bona. It lies on the Mediterranean fea, and there is a coral fifhery near it. It is a town of no importance, and of flender population. In this part of the world, elegant architecture, has, for many centuries been utterly forgotten or defpifed. The buildings of Bona, as every where elfe, are therefore mean. It is expofed to the incurfions of the Arabs. The name of this people is ufed by travellers in a very indefinite manner. Algiers is at the diftance of fome hundreds of leagues from Arabia: but as this part of Africa was formerly conquered by that nation, under the banners of Mahomet, the name is ftill applied to a race of tawny and independent barbarians, who wander in gangs about the country, and unite the double profeffions of a fhepherd and a robber. Bona was formerly a magnificent city. Its grandeur is now only to be traced in the ruins of a monaftery. It has a fortrefs, and a garrifon of three hundred Turks, as the banditti chufe to call themfelves; a Turk being the moft reputable title in that country. This circumftance is alone fufficient to afcertain the depth of its wretchednefs. Thefe adventurers however are not Turks, but the fweepings of all nations blended together. They are commanded by an aga, who is likewife governor of the town. Bona was taken by Charles V. in his expedition to Tunis, but was not long after recovered by its former masters.

Constantina is situated on the river Sef Gomar, forty eight miles from the sea-coast. It received its present name from that of a princess, the daughter of the emperor Constantine, to whom it was indebted for magnificence. The situation is on a peninsula, difficult of access, except towards the south.west. It is one mile in circumference, well fortified, and contains many fragments of ancient architecture. In particular there is part of a noble bridge; and near it, is a large subterraneous aqueduct, which terminates in a cascade. State criminals are sometimes precipitated down this place, and dashed to pieces against the rocks at its bottom. A bey resides here, and has under his command three hundred Turkish horse, and one thousand five hundred Moorish soldiers. This is the account given by travellers, though it is not likely that the number of the garrison is always the same. In details of this kind, we must be contented with the best materials that can be had, though sometimes not entirely above exception. The inhabitants of Constantina, are said to be opulent and haughty. This city was formerly the residence of a race of kings who governed the province of Constantina, of which it is the metropolis; but in the year 1520, the whole territory was conquered by Barbarossa, that distinguished scourge of mankind, who annexed it to the government of Algiers. Some splendid ruins exist in the vicinity of Constantina. Upon the sea-coast, at a small distance from it, are the traces of a Roman colony, antiently called Colo. It is situated on a high rock, and has a garrison. Adjoining to it is a French factory, to which the Moors bring hides, wax, and wool, for sale. At no great distance are the remains of the ancient city of Stora. It is said that the mountainous part of this territory is inhabited by a hardy people, who can raise forty thousand fighting men. It is not probable, that those writers who made this assertion had ever an opportunity of counting their number. History abounds with such random calculations. The vagabond who founded Rome has been supplied by the generosity of succeeding historians, with an army about equally numerous, though it is, at the same time, acknowledged, that his *kingdom* was only seven or eight miles in length.

Gigeri is situated about fifteen miles from Bona. It contains about fifteen hundred houses, and the inhabitants are very poor. It is defended by a fort and a small garrison. The natives of this part of the country are independent and barbarous. They retire, when circumstances require it, to inaccessible fastnesses, and set the dey of Algiers at defiance. Ships, when wrecked on this coast, are plundered, and the crews are treated with the utmost savageness. In this respect, however, the natives of the territory of Gigeri cannot differ much for the worse from the rest of their countrymen; nor is the practice peculiar to Barbary. Scenes of the same kind are frequently acted, and if any thing can be still more infamous, are almost always acted with impunity, on the coast of Cornwall, and other maritime counties of England.* The French, in the year 1666, had begun to fortify Gigeri. They were driven from it by the Algerines, with the loss of their cannon, and most of their effects.

Bugia, was formerly the capital of a kingdom of the same name. It stands at the mouth of the river Major, or Zinganor, about twenty leagues to the eastward of Algiers. It is little better than a heap of ruins; a description which applies to almost every town in that part of the world. It has three castles, two at the port, and one upon a rock, at a small distance behind them. In the year 1671, a British admiral took or destroyed, in this harbour, nine Algerine ships of war. It is extremely seldom, that an admiral has been charged with such a laudable commission.

Steffa or Steffa, is situated in a fertile valley, sixty miles to the south of Bugia, and fifteen miles from the sea. It exhibits only the melancholy ruins of its former

___

* There is a story of an English parson, whose congregation, during the time of divine service, heard of a shipwreck. In spite of his utmost efforts to detain them, the whole assembly rushed out of church, in a body, to divide the plunder.

magnificence, containing about three hundred miferable families.

Tebef was formerly a flourifhing city, but is at prefent extremely reduced. Zamoura is in the fame condition. It is defended by a fort. Couco was once the metropolis of a kingdom of the fame name. Its fovereigns were in the habit of forming alliances with the court of Spain. For this reafon, the Algerines, in the beginning of the feventeenth century, ravaged the whole country, and deftroyed every town in it. The inhabitants have ftill fupported their independence, by taking refuge in the mountainous parts of the country, which are faid to be very fertile; but the Algerines prevent them from holding any intercourfe with foreign nations. Bifcara, has a fort and garrifon. One of the chief employments of the people here, is to catch and tame lions, tygers, and other beafts of prey, which they carry for fale to Algiers. Necanz, is one of the pleafanteft towns in Barbary. It is watered by an agreeable river, whofe banks are adorned with a variety of beautiful trees. The town contains a magnificent mofque and a college for the education of Mahometan ftudents.

Oran is fituated about two hundred and fifty miles weft of Algiers. It lies partly on a plain, and partly on the afcent of a hill. It is a mile and an half in circumference and tolerably fortified. But it is unfortunately commanded by fome of the neigbouring eminences; fo that a garrifon of ten or twelve thoufand men is neceffary to defend it with fuccefs againft a fkilful enemy. As the Spanifh coafts and merchant fhips had fuffered much from the corfairs of this port, Ferdinand king of Spain, determined to attempt its reduction. For this purpofe, he tranfported into Africa an army, under the command of his prime minifter cardinal Ximenes, one of thofe few ftatefmen, who have not deferved the deteftation of mankind. The wonted good fortune of Ximenes, did not, at this juncture, defert him. He had maintained a correfpondence with fome of the people of Oran; and when the Moors fallied out to attack the Spanifh army, their perfidious countrymen fhut the gates againft them. Ximenes killed four thoufand of the barbarians, and fet at liberty twenty thoufand Chriftian flaves. The Algerines, during almoft two hundred years, made frequent and unfuccefsful attempts to recover the town. At laft, in 1708, they retook it. In June, 1732, a Spanifh army was difembarked not far from Oran. The Turkifh commander, his troops, and the inhabitants were feized with a panic, and abandoned their fortifications without much refiftance. The victors found in the place an hundred and forty fix pieces of cannon, befides mortars, and at leaft fifty fhip loads of provifions. This latter fupply contributed much to the prefervation of their new conqueft. Without it they muft have run the greateft hazard of perifhing in the midft of fuccefs; as a tempeft, which lafted for feveral days, cut off all intercourfe between the army upon fhore, and the fleet at fea. The Moors not long after attacked the Spaniards with great fury, but were finally repulfed with much flaughter on both fides. Oran is ftill poffeffed by Spain.

Tremefen was formerly the capital town of a kingdom of that name. It is fituated ninety miles fouth-weft of Oran, furrounded by a ftrong wall and well fortified. It has five gates with draw-bridges before them, and a caftle containing handfome barracks for the Janifaries who are in garrifon. Tremefen while a metropolis was a fplendid city. It contained one hundred and fifty mofques, and one hundred and fixty public baths. Since it ceafed to be the feat of an independent government, it hath fhrunk into ruins and defolation. The mofques are reduced to eight, and its public baths to four. The inhabitants are extremely indigent.

Moftagan, ftands fifty miles eaft of Oran. This town is built in the form of a theatre opening to the fea, and furrounded on every other fide with rocks that hang over it. The ruins of an old Moorifh caftle ftand in a fpace between the rocks, and there is a ftrong ftone wall towards the port, with a modern built caftle, garrifoned by a number of Turks. The citadel is erected upon the fummit of one of the rocks, and commands both city and territory. The haven is commodious, and the town is well fupplied with water. The neigh

bouring mountains are inhabited by a people called
Magarabas, who live in tents, posses a great number
of flocks, and pay to the dey of Algiers twelve thousand crowns annually. There is a handsome mosque in
this town.

Tenez, is situated about one hundred miles to the
eastward of Oran, twenty miles east of Mostagan, and
at a league distant from the sea, where it has a convenient
port. There is a castle that was once a royal palace,
and in which the governor resides. The fortifications
are strong, the garrison numerous, and the neighbouring territory fertile. This was supposed to have been
the Julia Cæsarea of the ancients.

Sercelli, lies between Tenez and Algiers, about twenty four miles to the westward of the latter. It is defended by a Turkish garrison, and has a port, which
will only admit of small vessels. This was antiently a
large and populous city, but is at present a poor and
desolate place.

The southern part of the Algerine territories, is inhabited by a wandering race of people, who like the
Tartars, roam from place to place, and live in tents.
The country itself is hilly, a branch of mount Atlas run-
ning through it. The only riches of the people are
their numerous flocks and herds. The government
exacts a tribute from them, but a bey is obliged to
come annually at the head of an army to collect it;
and many of them retire to inaccessible places till the
troops are withdrawn, in order to evade the payment.

Algiers, itself stands on a bay of the Mediterranean
sea. It is built on the side of a mountain. The houses
rise gradually from the sea-shore up the ascent, in the
form of an amphitheatre. The town appears beautiful
at a distance, when approaching from the water. The
mosques, castles, and other public buildings have a
striking effect; but the streets are narrow, and the
houses mean. The roofs are flat, so that the people can
visit each other, at a considerable distance in the town
without going into the streets. The walls are about a
league in circumference, and defended by some square
towers and bastions. The port has a pier about five

hundred paces in length, which extends from the continent to a small rocky island called the Lantern. On this island, there is a castle with three lines of brass cannon. The town has five gates, ten great mosques, and fifty lesser ones, and is computed to contain an hundred thousand inhabitants. The fortifications are extensive and strong. The Christian slaves are often employed in removing stones from a quarry, at some distance in the country, which they lay on the sand, to defend the mole from the impetuosity of the waves. This laborious work is never at an end, because the sea constantly washes away the stones, and makes a perpetual supply necessary. One street, which is broad and handsome, passes through the town from east to west; but all the other streets are narrow, incommodious, and dirty. There are said to be fifteen thousand houses, which are commonly built round a small square with a paved court in the centre. Around this court is a double range of galleries, one above the other, and both supported by columns. The palace of the dey stands in the centre of the city. This building is very extensive, and surrounded by two superb galleries, supported by marble pillars. There is a law here, by which any woman convicted of amorous correspondence with a Christian, is thrown into the sea, with her head tied up in a sack, unless her lover chuses to turn Mahometan. Examples of this kind are not unfrequent, as the fair sex, in that part of the world, are said to be remarkably frail. Six of the baths have been converted into prisons for the Christian slaves. In each of these, there is a chapel for the free exercise of their religion. Every slave is let out at a certain hour in the morning, and must return at a stated hour at night, in order to be locked up. Each of them is allowed a matrass and a rug for a bed. There are several tolerable edifices without the walls of the town, which add to the beauty of the environs. Among these are a variety of Turkish sepulchres and monuments. One of these monuments contains six magnificent tombs of a circular figure. They were erected to the memory of six deys, who were in the course of a few days, successively elected and murdered.

There is perhaps no nation in the world from which we may not learn fome ufeful leffon. With refpect to the burial of their dead, travellers inform us, that the Mahometans difcover a degree of delicacy of which Chriftians have no conception. In our church yards, nothing is more common, and furely nothing can be more completely fhocking, than to fee graves broke up, a fecond time, before the perfon has returned to his original duft; and the remains of the dead are toffed about with as little ceremony as poffible. This wretched violation of decency arifes from the orthodox defire of being buried in holy ground; a practice which has no doubt been encouraged by the parties concerned, for the purpofe of exacting a high price. Exorbitant demands of this kind have not long fince been paid within lefs than an hundred miles of Philadelphia. The Algerines, and the other profeffors of the Mahometan religion, would regard it as an act of the moft barbarous facrilege to difturb the remains of the dead, by opening their graves, at any diftance of time, or upon any pretence whatever. Hence their burial grounds in the neighbourhood of a large city are fometimes ten miles in extent.

Algiers had formerly nothing but rain water. A Moor, who had been driven from Spain, conftructed two aqueducts, by which it is now fupplied with abundance of excellent water from the adjacent mountains. The country around this city is very fertile. Country-feats, gardens, and groves of trees are faid to be numerous. The Algerines are unacquainted with the art of pruning and grafting trees. Their gardens are not walled, but fenced round with a peculiar fpecies of fig-trees, which from their prickles, and the compactnefs with which their branches interweave, are well adapted for that purpofe. Among other rich tracts in the province of Algiers Proper, the great plain of Mettijah is admired for its aftonifhing fertility. It is fifty miles in length, twenty in breadth, and includes many villas, fragrant groves, and delightful gardens. The foil produces fuch a profufion of the moft delicious fruits, rice, roots, and grain of every fpecies, that the inhabitants enjoy annually two, and frequently three

B

crops The hot baths of Meereega, in the neighbourhood of this city, are natural curiosities. The principal
one is twelve feet square and four deep. The water is
very hot, and when it has filled the larger bason, runs
through it into another of a smaller size, where the Jews
bathe, as they are not permitted to use the same bath,
with the Mahometans. These hot fountains are conjec-
tured to proceed from the great quantities of sulphur,
nitre, and other inflammable substances in the bowels
of the earth. To this cause likewise have been ascribed
those earthquakes, to which the whole country, and Algiers in particular, are frequently subjected.

CHAPTER II.

Customs. Religion. Government. Land Forces. Corsairs.

THE present inhabitants of the territory of Algiers
are composed of a multitude of different nations.
Among these are the Moors or Morescos who were driven
out of Spain about the end of the sixteenth century,
and the Arabians, who trace their descent from those
disciples of Mahomet who formerly subdued this country. Levantines, Turks, Jews, and Christian slaves, with
a croud formed of the posterity of all these different
people, make up the rest of the population. The Moors
and Arabs are the most numerous. The former
compose the great body of the inhabitants of the towns.
But it may be readily supposed, that amidst such a variety of different races, immense numbers cannot be
said to belong to any particular tribe or nation whatever. In this country there are many wandering bands
of shepherds, who live together in camps and remove
from one place to another as they want pasture for their
herds and flocks, or as any other accidental circumstance
happens to make it necessary. They sometimes pay
rent to landlords, in corn, fruit, honey, wax, and other
productions of the same kind. The dey likewise demands a tribute. The excellence of the climate ren-
ders this simple way of living tolerable, though the
tents of these people are mean, their utensils of little

value, and their lodging filthy. The family and their
domeftic animals, lie promifcuoufly in the tents together, except the dogs, which are left on the outfide
as guards. They raife confiderable numbers of bees
and of filk-worms. They fubfift chiefly on bread, rice
and fruit. Wine and fpirituous liquors are almoft entirely unknown.

The drefs of the men is only a long piece of coarfe
cloth wrapped round the fhoulders, and falling down to
their ankles, with a cap of the fame ftuff. The women
pay fome more attention to the ornamental part of
drefs. The children are fuffered to go ftark naked
till feven or eight years of age. The Sheik or chief
of a tribe wears a cap of fine cloth. Thefe people are
ufually called Arabs; their cuftoms, language and religion bear a ftrict affinity with thofe of Arabia. They
are robuft and of a fwarthy complexion. The men are
active, the women prolific, and the children healthy.
They have neither to encounter the hardfhips incident
to the life of a North-American favage, nor are their
conftitutions enfeebled, as is fometimes the cafe in ma-
nufacturing towns, by fedentary and unhealthful employments. When a young man would marry, he
drives a number of cattle to the hut where the parents
of his miftrefs refide. The bride is fet on horfeback
and led home, amidft the fhouts of a croud of young
people, who have been invited to the nuptial feaft.
When fhe arrives at the hut of her lover, a mixture of
milk and honey is given her to drink, and a fong fuitable to the occafion is fung. She then alights, and is
prefented with a ftick, which fhe thrufts into the ground,
and repeats fome lines to the followiug effect: " As
" this ftick is faftened in the earth, fo I am in duty
" bound to my hufband; as nothing but violence can
" remove it, fo death alone fhall force me from his
" love." She then drives his flock to water and back
again, to fhew her willingnefs to perform any duty that
he may affign her. Thefe previous ceremonies being
fettled, all the company enter the hut, and the evening
concludes with the greateft feftivity that thefe people are
capable of enjoying. Subfequent to the marriage, the

wife is obliged to wear a vail. She never ſtirs from the hut for the ſpace of a month, after that time. Theſe are the ceremonies reported to be cuſtomary in celebrating a marriage among the paſtoral tribes of Barbary. But narratives of this kind muſt be received, as biſhop Burnet admoniſhes the reader, to peruſe his Hiſtory of his own times, viz. *with ſome grains of allowance.* Such uniform regularity is hardly to be expected among a race of wandering ſhepherds. Perhaps an African critic would turn from our deſcription of his country with as much diſdain, as a citizen of the United States feels in attempting to peruſe a frothy volume reſpecting North-America, fabricated by ſome of the profeſſional book-builders of Paris or of London.*

* The following curious circumſtances may ſerve to ſhew what kind of opinion ought to be entertained of the authors of oriental travels. In the year 1783, an adventurer, who called himſelf a modern Greek, publiſhed a ſmall volume entitled *the life of Ali Bey.* It contained ſome romantic ſtories, which the author atteſted as an eye witneſs. About this time the court of France had diſpatched into Egypt Monſieur Savary, a gentleman of ſome note in the republic of letters. His buſineſs was to obtain authentic information concerning the ancient and modern ſituation of that country. He returned, and in due time publiſhed two large volumes, pregnant with learning and ſublimity. Monſieur Volney ſoon after entered the liſts as a third champion. He made a very ſevere attack on the veracity of his French predeceſſor. In particular, he upbraided him with having ſtolen a great number of pages, from a very contemptible impoſture which pretended to be a *life of Ali Bey.* This biographer, as an evidence, perhaps, of his claſſical pedigree, had aſſumed the name of *Coſmopolitos.* Volney added that a copy of the book having by chance come to Egypt, while he was there, the European merchants in that province could not help expreſſing their ſurprize, that their countrymen were ſtupid enough to digeſt ſuch ridiculous reveries. Monſieur Savary did not long ſurvive this humiliating diſcovery. But the " Modern Greek" replied in a volume of letters, which he inſcribed by permiſſion to ſir William Fordyce, an eminent Engliſh phyſician. In this work he affirms that Volney himſelf wrote HIS travels *in a garret at London.* BELLA! HORRIDA BELLA!

It is certainly, though not generally known, that the letters

The Moors or Arabs, for the two names appear to be synonymous, are good horsemen, but great thieves. Their principal arms are a short lance and a scymitar, though they are likewise acquainted with the bow and the musket. It is dangerous to travel in the country, for fear of being robbed, but persons are said to be in safety, if attended by one of the Mahometan Marabouts or hermits. The inhabitants on the sea-coast are perfectly versant in the use of fire-arms.

Algiers retains the title of a kingdom, an epithet which might, without regret, be expunged from every human vocabulary. It is however a military republic, though it certainly can reflect no lustre on that species of government. The national ordinances run in these words: " We, the great, and small members of the " mighty and invincible militia of Algiers," &c. The dey is elected by a divan composed from the army. He seldom secures his office, without tumult and bloodshed ; and he often falls by the dagger of an assassin. This sovereign may with peculiar propriety adopt the expression of one of the heroes of Ossian : " I was born in " the midst of battles, and my steps must move in blood " to the tomb." The way in which his authority is exercised, corresponds with that by which it has been obtained. When Mr. Bruce, as British resident at Algiers, had occasion to visit the dey, he sometimes found him in his hall of audience, with his cloaths all bespattered with blood, like those of a carcase butcher. It is a very frequent amusement with him, to cause the heads of his subjects to be struck off in his presence. Mr. Bruce said, that he knew of one man, who was executed, for no greater offence than because a gunflint was found upon him. His indictment and trial were very concise. " You rascal, what business have

of lady Mary Wortley Montague are the offspring of a mercantile pen. Even Baron Tott, and Mr. Bruce, though writers of *comparative* authenticity, require in the reader, strong and frequent doses of faith.

" you with a flint, unlefs you were going to confpire
" againft the ftate ?"*

The aga of the Janiffaries is the officer next to the
dey in dignity and power. He enjoys his poft but two
months, and then retires upon a penfion. The other
officers of importance are a fecretary of ftate, twenty
four Chiah baffas or colonels fubordinate to the aga,
eight hundred fenior captains, and four hundred lieu-
tenants. Among thefe officers, the right of feniority
is ftrictly obferved. A breach of this point would be
expected to produce a revolt among the foldiers, and
might perhaps coft the dey his life. Befides thefe officers, there are others belonging to the Turkifh forces,
who form a feparate body. The dey has a corps of
guards ; a very neceffary, though fometimes a fruitlefs
precaution; as any private foldier who has the
courage to murder him, ftands an equal chance of
becoming his fucceffor. Experiments of this defcription are fometimes made. Since the beginning
of the prefent century, fix private foldiers entered into
a confpiracy to kill a dey of one of the ftates of Barbary. They gave him a mortal wound in his palace, and
in the midft of a croud of people. He expired, ex-
claiming, " Has nobody the courage to kill a villain?"
One of the confpirators, the intended fucceffor, inftantly afcended the vacant throne, and brandifhing his naked
fcymitar, declared *that he would do juftice to all!* His
five affociates went about the hall to inforce the title of
their new mafter ; and none prefent feemed to give
themfelves any difturbance about what had happened.
He kept his fituation unmolefted, for about ten minutes, till an old veteran unobferved took aim with a
mufket or blunderbufs, and fhot him dead. Upon this,
the five others were immediately difpatched by the perfons prefent. But what fhewed the nature of the government in its proper light was the obfervation of the
new dey. He faid, that if the ufurper could have held

* Thefe picturefque details are not inferted in the publica-
tion of Mr. Bruce; but they were related to me on his authority, by a gentleman of the firft rank in the literary world.

his place for twenty minutes longer, he would have obtained the throne.

The people of Algiers in general speak a compound of Arabic, Morefco, and the remains of the ancient Phœnician languages. The natives of all denominations, for the moſt part, underſtand the *Lingua Franca*. This is a kind of dialect, which without being the proper language of any country on the coaſt of the Mediterranean ſea, has a kind of univerſal currency all over that quarter of the world, as the channel of information, for people, who cannot underſtand each other through any medium but itſelf. The public buſineſs of the nation is tranſacted in the Turkiſh tongue, in which alſo the records are kept. It is curious, that in converſation, a Turk tranſpoſes his nouns and verbs, in the ſame way that the Greek and Latin writers have done. Some of our modern critics have been woefully perplexed in attempting to explain this practice, which they ſeem to conſider as peculiar to thoſe two ancient languages. Had they been acquainted with the circumſtance juſt now mentioned, they might readily have ſolved ſome of their doubts, by a voyage to Conſtantinople.

In Algiers, both men and women ſpend a great part of their time in indolence; the men, in drinking coffee and ſmoaking; and the women, in dreſſing, bathing, viſiting the tombs of their relations, and ſauntering in their gardens. The Algerines by their law may have four wives, but they uſually content themſelves with two or three at the moſt. The huſband ſeldom fees his wife before marriage, but accepts her upon the deſcription of a female confident. When the match is agreed upon, the bridegroom ſends a preſent of fruits and ſweetmeats to the bride, and entertains her relations with a feaſt and a muſical entertainment.*

---

* An author, whoſe bulk at leaſt entitles him to reſpect, gravely tells us, that when an Algerine dies, his body is clad in a turban, a ſhirt, a pair of drawers, and *a ſilk robe!* If we underſtand this paſſage in its literal ſenſe, ſilk muſt be more abundant, in that kingdom, than linen is, in any part of Europe; ſince it is certain that thouſands of poor people in Europe are buried without even a ſhirt. Thus it is that books of

The militia who elect the dey are either Turks or renegado Christians. Their number has been variously stated by different authors from six thousand five hundred to twelve thousand. The dey pays no other revenue to the grand seignior, than that of a certain number of handsome youths, and some other annual presents. His income is more or less in proportion to his opportunities of plundering his neighbours or his subjects. Dr Shaw says, that the taxes of the whole kingdom produce yearly to the dey but about three hundred thousand dollars. He conjectures that the eighth share of the prizes, the property of persons who die without children, and to whom the dey falls heir, with the presents from foreign nations, and his private acts of robbery at home, extend to an equal sum. It is easy to see that this calculation must be extremely questionable. The tyrant himself can hardly be supposed capable to give a distinct estimate.

The Mufti, the Cadi, and the grand Marabout, are the principal ecclesiastics. The first is the high priest of their religion ; the second, the supreme judge in ecclesiastical causes, and in such civil matters as the civil power does not interpose in. The third is the chief of an order of saints or hermits. These three persons are distinguished by the largeness of their turbans. They sit in the divan a little below the dey, on his right hand. The divan itself consists of about two thousand Turkish officers and soldiers.

The common punishment at Algiers, for offences not capital, is the bastinado ; for those, which are so, the bow-string, which two people pull different ways with all their strength, so that the criminal is instantly dispatched. The Christian slaves are liable to a variety of punishments. They are sometimes burned, or rather roasted alive. At other times, they are impaled. This is done, by placing the offender on the

travels are written. The journalist records what he has seen happen once, or perhaps has never seen at all, as what takes place every day. The writer above referred to might as well have told us, that every native of Algiers was seven feet high.

of a fharp ftake, which is thruft up his pofteriors clofe by the back-bone, till it appears above his fhoulders. Slaves are fometimes caft over the walls of a town upon iron hooks. Thefe catch by the jaws, by the ribs, or fome other part of the body; and the fufferers have been known to hang thus for feveral days, alive, and in the moft exquifite torture. Crucifixion, by nailing the hands and feet to walls, is likewife practifed.

A Moor convicted of houfe-breaking, hath his right hand cut off and faftened about his neck. He is then led through the city on an afs, with his face towards its tail. Perfons of diftinction, for crimes againft the ftate, are placed between two boards, and fawed afunder. Women, detected in adultery, are fixed by their necks to a pole, and held under water till they are fuffocated.

When an Algerine pirate takes a prize, he examines into the quality and circumftances of the prifoners. If he difbelieves the account that they give of themfelves, they are baftinadoed, till he has met with an agreeable anfwer. Having obtained what information he is able, he brings them on fhore, after having ftripped them almoft naked. He carries them directly to the palace of the dey, where the European confuls affemble, to fee if any of the prifoners belong to their refpective nations, who are at peace with Algiers. In that cafe, they reclaim them, provided that they were only paffengers; but if they have ferved on board of the fhips of any people at war with " the mighty and invincible " militia," they cannot be difcharged without payment of the full ranfom.

Matters are thus fettled between the dey and the confuls, what part of the prifoners are to be fet at liberty, and what part are to be confidered as flaves. The dey has next his choice of every eighth flave. He generally chufes the mafters, furgeons, carpenters, and moft ufeful hands belonging to the feveral prizes. Befides his eighth, he lays claim to all prifoners of quality, for whom a fuperior ranfom is to be expected. The reft are left to the corfair and his owners. They are carried to the flave market; the crier proclaims their

C

rank, profeffion, and circumftances, and the price fet
upon each of them. They are then led to the court
before the palace of the dey, and there fold to the beft
bidder. If any fum is offered beyond the price firft
fet upon them, it belongs to the government. The
captors and owners have only that which was originally
fet upon the flaves. For this practice of buying and
felling flaves, we are not entitled to charge the Algerines
with any exclufive degree of barbarity. The Chriftians
of Europe and America carry on this commerce an
hundred times more extenfively than the Algerines. It
has received a recent fanction from the immaculate
Divan of Britain. Nobody feems even to be furprifed
by a diabolical kind of advertifements, which, for fome
months paft, have frequently adorned the newfpapers of
Philadelphia. The French fugitives from the Weft-In-
dies have brought with them a croud of flaves. Thefe
moft injured people fometimes run off, and their mafter
advertifes a reward for apprehending them. At the
fame time, we are commonly informed, that his facred
name is marked in capitals, on their breafts; or in
plainer terms, it is ftamped on that part of the body
with a red hot iron. Before therefore we reprobate the
ferocity of the Algerines, we fhould enquire whether it
is not poffible to find, in fome other regions of the
globe, a fyftematic brutality ftill more difgraceful?

CHAPTER III.

*Origin of the prefent government of Algiers. Expedi-
dition of Charles V.*

ALGIERS had undergone a variety of revolutions
in its form of government, previous to the beginning of the fixteenth century, which it is not within the
plan of this fketch to defcribe. But about that time, a
fudden revolution happened, which, by rendering the
ftates of Barbary formidable to the Europeans, hath made
their hiftory worthy of more attention. " This revolution was brought about, by perfons born in a rank

⁴ of life, which entitled them to act no such *illuſtrious*
" part."* Horuc and Hayradin, the ſons of a potter

* Robertſon's Hiſtory of Charles V. book 5. It is to be
wiſhed, that this writer had left us an explanation of what idea
he intended to convey, by the word *illuſtrious*. In his Hiſtory
of America, it is frequently applied to the conquerors of Mexi-
co and Peru ; and here to the founders of the piratical ſtate of
Algiers. Yet a few lines farther down, in the page juſt quoted,
he ſays, that theſe corſairs, whom he had juſt before termed
illuſtrious, followed an *infamous* trade. Immediately after, he
charges one of them with a perfidious *murther*. If theſe are
not contradictions, what name are we to give them? In the
hiſtory of America, book 5, he tells us that Cortes "has been
" *admired* and *celebrated* by ſucceeding ages." Thus a pres-
byterian divine holds forth as an object of *admiration* and *ce-
lebrity*, the butcher of two or three millions of innocent people:
Dr. Robertſon has filled three octavo volumes, with a hiſtory
of the reign of Charles V. who was likewiſe, it ſeems, an object
worthy of *admiration*. This tyrant conſigned to the execu-
tioner, fifty or an hundred thouſand of his proteſtant ſubjects
in the Netherlands ; as we are informed by father Paul and
Grotius. There is not, however, to be found, in the narrative of the panegyriſt of Barbaroſſa, one ſingle word of ſuch
a bloody perſecution ; nor has this ſtupendous mutilation of
hiſtory been ſtarted as an objection to Dr. Robertſon, by any
of the London critics, whom I have met with. Had this re-
verend author been writing the life of Richard III. of England, we may, from what has been above ſtated, conjecture,
that he would have forgot to mention the two nephews of
that *illuſtrious* ſovereign. Of ſuch heroes, ſuch an encomiaſt,
and a world that admires the one and the other, candour can
only ſay, *Malus, Pejor, Peſſimus.*

It is provoking to ſee how many of the moſt diſtinguiſhed
hiſtorians deſpiſe the reputation of veracity. Mr. Hume, as a
pattern of excellence, is uſually coupled with Dr. Robertſon.
As to him, the reader may look into my additions to the article
of IRELAND, in the American edition of Guthrie's geography.
In this reſpect, the ancients are often as exceptionable. Salluſt
pronounces for Catiline, a long ſpeech to his army, juſt before
its defeat. He adds, ſoon after, *Poſtremo, ex omni copia, neque
in prœlio, neque in fuga, quisquam civis ingenuus captus eſt.* From
this expreſſion we are to underſtand, that the whole rebel army
was cut to pieces; a few fugitive ſlaves perhaps excepted.
Where then did Salluſt obtain a copy of the ſpeech of Cata-
line ? or what are we to think as to the fidelity of that moſt
enchanting writer?

in the ifle of Lefbos, prompted by a reftlefs and enter-
prifing fpirit, forfook their father's profeffion, ran to
fea, and joined a crew of pirates. They foon diftin-
guifhed themfelves by their valour and activity, and
becoming matters of a fmall brigantine, fupported their
infamous trade with fuch conduct and fuccefs, that they
affembled a fleet of twelve galleys, befides many veffels
of fmaller force. Of this fleet, Horuc, the elder brother, called Barbaroffa from the red colour of his beard,
was admiral, and Hayradin fecond in command. Their
names foon became terrible from the Straits of the Dar-
danelles to thofe of Gibraltar. Together with their
power their ambitious views extended, and while acting
as corfairs, they affumed the ideas, and acquired the
talents of conquerors. They often carried the prizes,
which they took on the coaft of Spain and Italy, into
the ports of Barbary. The convenient fituation of
thefe harbours, lying fo near the greateft commercial
ftates at that time in Chriftendom, made the brothers
wifh for an eftablifhment in that country. An opportunity of accomplifhing this project, prefented itfelf,
and they did not fuffer it to pafs unimproved. Eutemi,
king of Algiers, having attempted feveral times, without fuccefs, to take a fort which the Spanifh governors
of Oran had built not far from his capital, applied to
Barbaroffa. The corfair, leaving his brother Hayradin
with the fleet, marched at the head of five thoufand
men to Algiers. Such a force gave him the command
of the town. He fecretly murdered the monarch whom
he had come to affift, and proclaimed himfelf king in
his ftead. The authority which he had ufurped, he
eftablifhed by arts fuited to the genius of the people
whom he had to govern ; by liberality without bounds
to thofe who favoured his promotion, and by cruelty
no lefs unbounded to all whom he had any reafon to
miftruft. He continued to infeft the coaft of Spain and
Italy with fleets which refembled the armaments of a
great monarch, rather than the fquadrons of a pirate.
Their frequent and cruel devaftations obliged Charles
V. about the beginning of his reign, to furnifh the
Marquis de Comares, governor of Oran, with troops

sufficient to attack him. That officer executed the commission with such spirit, that Barbarossa's forces being vanquished in several encounters, he himself was shut up in Tremecen, and in attempting to make his escape was fortunately slain.

His brother Hayradin, known likewise by the name of Barbarossa, assumed the sceptre of Algiers. He carried on his naval robberies with great vigour, and extended his conquests on the continent of Africa. But perceiving that the Moors and Arabs submitted to his government with the utmost reluctance, and being afraid that his continual depredations would, one day, draw upon him the arms of the Christians, he put his dominions under the protection of the grand seignior, and received from him a body of Turkish soldiers sufficient for his security against his domestic as well as foreign enemies. At last, the infamy, or, as Dr. Robertson calls it, the *fame* of his exploits daily increasing, Solyman offered him the command of the Turkish fleet; and Hayradin on the other hand, justly dreading the consequences of the tyranny of his officers over the Algerines, sought the protection of the grand seignior. This was readily granted, and himself appointed bashaw or viceroy of Algiers; by which means he received such considerable reinforcements, that the unhappy Algerines durst not make the least complaint; and such numbers of Turks resorted to him, that he was not only capable of keeping the Moors and Arabs in subjection at home, but of annoying the Christians at sea.

Hayradin set about building a strong mole for the safety of his ships. In this he employed thirty thousand Christian slaves, whom he obliged to work without intermission for three years, in which time the work was completed. Hayradin soon became dreaded not only by the Arabs and Moors, but also by the maritime Christian powers, especially the Spaniards. The viceroy failed not to acquaint the grand seignior with his success, and obtained from him a fresh supply of money, by which he was enabled to build strong forts, and to erect batteries on all places that might favour the landing of an enemy. All these have since received greater improvements from time to time, as often as there was occasion for them.

In the mean time the sultan, either out of a sense of the great services of Hayradin, or perhaps out of jealousy left he should make himself independent, raised him to the dignity of bashaw of the empire, and appointed Haffan-Aga, a Sardinian renegado, to succeed him as bashaw of Algiers. Haffan had no sooner taken possession of his new government, than he began to pursue his ravages on the Spanish coast with greater fury than ever; extending them to the ecclefiastical state, and other parts of Italy. Pope Paul III. alarmed at this proceeding, exhorted the emperor Charles V. to send a powerful fleet to suppress those frequent piracies; and, that nothing might be wanting to render the enterprize successful, a bull was published by his holiness, wherein a plenary absolution of sins, and the crown of martyrdom, were promised to all those who either fell in battle or were made slaves. The emperor, on his part, needed no incitement, and therefore set sail at the head of a powerful fleet, consisting of an hundred and twenty ships and twenty gallies, having on board thirty thousand troops, with an immense quantity of arms, and ammunition. In this expedition, many young nobility and gentlemen attended as volunteers, and among these many knights of Malta, so remarkable for their valour against the enemies of Christianity. Even ladies of birth and character attended Charles, and the wives and daughters of the officers and soldiers followed him with a design to settle in Barbary, after the conquest was finished.

By this prodigious armament the Algerines were thrown into the utmost consternation. The city was surrounded only by a wall with scarce any out-works. The garrison consisted of eight hundred Turks and six thousand Moors, without fire-arms, and poorly disciplined and accoutred; the rest of their forces being dispersed in the other provinces of the kingdom, to levy the usual tribute on the Arabs and Moors. The Spaniards landed without opposition, and immediately built a fort, under the cannon of which they encamped, and diverted the courfe of a fpring which fupplied the city with water. Being now reduced to the utmoft diftrefs, Haffan received a fummons to furrender at difcretion, on pain of being put to the fword with all his garrifon. The herald was ordered to extoll the vaft power of the emperor both by fea and land, and to exhort him to return to the Chriftian religion. But to this Haffan only replied, that he muft be a madman, who would pretend to advife an enemy, and that the perfon advifed would act ftill more madly who would take counfel of fuch an advifer. He was, however, on the point of furrendering the city, when intelligence wat brought him that the forces belonging to the weftern government were in full march towards the place ; upon which it was refolved to defend it to the utmoft. Charles, in the mean time, refolving upon a general affault, kept a conftant firing on the town ; which, from the weak defence made by the garrifon, he looked upon as already in his hands. But while the divan were deliberating on the moft proper means of obtaining an honourable capitulation, a mad prophet, attended by a multitude of people, entered the affembly, and foretold the deftruction of the Spaniards before the end of the moon, exhorting the inhabitants to hold out till that time. This prediction was foon accomplifhed in a very furprifing and unexpected manner; for, on the 28th of October 1541, a dreadful ftorm of wind, rain, and hail, arofe from the north, accompanied with violent fhocks of earthquakes, and a difmal and univerfal darknefs both by fea and land ; fo that the fun, moon, and elements, feemed to combine together for the deftruction of the Spaniards. In that one night, fome fay in lefs than half an hour, eighty fix fhips and fifteen gallies were deftroyed, with all their crews and military ftores ; by which the army on fhore was deprived of all means of fubfiftence. Their camp alfo, which fpread itfelf along the plain under their fort, was laid quite under water by the torrents which defcended from the neighbouring hills. Many of the troops, by trying to remove into fome better fituation, were cut to pieces by the Moors and Arabs; while several gallies, and other veffels, endeavouring to gain fome neighbouring creeks along the coaft, were immediately plundered, and their crews maffacred by the inhabitants.

Next morning, Charles beheld the fea covered with the fragments of fhips, and the bodies of men, horfes, and other creatures, fwimming on the waves; at which he was fo difheartened, that abandoning his tents, artillery, and all his heavy baggage, to the enemy, he marched at the head of his army, in no fmall diforder, towards Cape Mallabux, in order to reimbark in thofe veffels, which had out-weathered the ftorm. But Haffan, who had watched his motions, allowed him juft time to get to the fhore, when he rallied out, and attacked the Spanians in the midft of their hurry to get into their fhips. He killed great numbers, and brought away a ftill greater number of captives; after which he returned in triumph to Algiers.

Soon after this, the prophet Yufef, who had foretold the deftruction of the Spaniards, was declared the deliverer of his country, and had a confiderable gratuity decreed him, with the liberty of exercifing his prophetic function unmolefted. It was not long, however, before the Marabouts, and fome interpreters of the law, made a ftrong oppofition againft him, remonftrating to the bafhaw, how ridiculous and fcandalous it was to their nation, to afcribe its deliverance to a poor fortune-teller, which had been obtained by the fervent prayers of an eminent faint of their own profeffion. But though the bafhaw and his divan feemed out of policy, to give into this laft notion, yet the impreffion, which the prediction of Yufef and its accomplifhment had made upon the minds of the common people, proved too ftrong to be eradicated; and the fpirit of divination and conjuring has fince got into fuch credit among them, that not only their great ftatefmen, but their priefts, marabouts, and fantoons, have applied themfelves to that ftudy, and dignified it with the name of Mahomet's Revelations.

The Spaniards had fcarce reached their fhips, when they were attacked by a frefh ftorm, in which fevera

more of them perished. A veffel in particular, conta-ui
ing feven hundred foldiers, befides failors, funk in the
fight of Charles, without a poffibility of faving a fingle
man. At length with much labour, they reached the
port of Bujeyah. They ftayed no longer here than till
the fixteenth of November, when they fet fail for Carthagena, and reached it on the twenty-fifth of the fame
month. In this unfortunate expedition upwards of one
hundred and twenty fhips and gallies were loft, with
above three hundred colonels and other officers, and eight
thoufand foldiers and marines, befides thofe deftroyed by the enemy on their reimbarkation, or drown-
ed in the laft ftorm. The number of prifoners was fo
great, that the Algerines fold fome of them, by way of
contempt, for an onion per head.

From this time, the Spaniards were never able to an-
noy the Algerines, in any confiderable degree. In 1555,
they loft the city of Bujeyah, which was taken by Salab
Bais, fucceffor to Haffan. This commander, in 1556,
fet out upon a new expedition, fufpected to be againft
Oran; but he was fcarcely got four leagues from Algiers, when the plague, which at that time raged vio-
lently in the city, broke out in his groin, and luckily
carried him off in twenty-four hours.

Immediately after his death, the Algerine foldiery
chofe a Corfican renegado, Haffan Corfo, in his room,
till they fhould receive further orders from the porte.
He did not accept of the bafhawfhip without a good
deal of difficulty, but immediately profecuted the intended expedition againft Oran, difpatching a meffenger
to acquaint the porte with what had happened. The
army had hardly begun their hoftilities againft the place,
when orders came from the porte, exprefsly forbidding
Haffan Corfo to begin the fiege, or, if he had begun it,
enjoining him to raife it immediately, which he accordingly did.

Corfo had enjoyed his dignity for four months, when
Tekelli, a new bafhaw, arrived, as his fucceffor from
Conftantinople. The Algerines refolved not to admit
him; but by the treachery of the Levantine foldiers, he
at laft entered. Corfo was thrown over a wall, in which

D

a number of iron hooks were fixed. One of thefe catching the ribs of his fide, he hung three days in horrid agony, before he expired. " We meet with " events in the annals of mankind, that make us doubt " the truth of the moft authentic hiftory. We cannot " believe that fuch actions have ever been committed " by the inhabitants of this globe, and by creatures of " the fame fpecies with ourfelves. We are tempted to " think we are perufing the records of hell."*

Tekelli was affaffinated under the dome of a faint, by Yufef Calabres, the favourite renegado of Haffan Corfo. The murderer was chofen bafhaw, but died of the plague, fix days after his election.

Yufef was fucceeded by Haffan the fon of Hayradin Barbaroffa. Not long after, the Spaniards undertook an expedition againft Moftagan under the command of the count d'Alcandela ; but were utterly defeated, the commander himfelf killed, and twelve thoufand men taken prifoners. Haffan having difobliged his fubjects,they fent him in irons to Conftantinople, while two Turkifh officers fupplied his place. Haffan cleared himfelf; but Achmet, a new bafhaw, was appointed. Upon his arrival at Algiers, he fent the two deputy bafhaws to Conftantinople, where their heads were ftruck off. Achmet, in four months died ; and Haffan was fent a third time viceroy to Algiers.

He foon engaged in the fiege of Marfalquiver,poffeffed by the Spaniards, and fituated near the city of Oran. The Turkifh ftandards were feveral times planted on the walls, and as often diflodged; but in the end Haffan was obliged to raife the fiege.

In 1567, Haffan was again recalled to Conftantinople. His fucceffor, Mahomet, incorporated the Janifaries and Levantine Turks together. He thus put an end to their diffentions, and laid the foundation of the Algerine independency on the porte. He likewife added fome confiderable fortifications to the city and caftle, which he defigned to render impregnable. At this time, one

* View of Society and Manners in Italy, by Dr. Moore. Letter 16th.

John Gafcon, a bold Spanifh adventurer, formed a defign of furprifing the whole piratic navy in the bay, and fetting them on fire in the night time. He had the permiffion of Philip II. and was furnifhed by him with veffels, mariners, and fire-works, for the execution of his plan. He fet fail for Algiers in the beginning of October, when moft, if not all the fhips lay at anchor there ; and advanced near enough, unfufpected, to view them. He came accordingly, unperceived by any, to the very mole gate, and difpatched his men with their fire-works ; but thefe were fo ill mixed, that they could not be kindled. Gafcon finding himfelf difcovered, and in the utmoft danger, failed away with all poffible hafte ; but he was purfued, overtaken, and brought back a prifoner. Mahomet immediately caufed a gibbet to be erected on the fpot where Gafcon had landed, and hung him by the feet upon a hook, with his royal commiffion tied to his toes. He had not been long fufpended, when the captain who made him prifoner, and a number of other corfairs, interceded fo ftrongly in his behalf, that he was taken down, and put under the care of fome Chriftian furgeons ; but two days after, fome Moors having reported as the common talk and belief in Spain, that the Algerines durft not hurt a hair of Gafcon's head, he was hoifted up by a pulley to the top of the execution wall, and thrown down again. In his fall, a hook catched him by the belly, and gave him a wound, of which he inftantly expired.

Mahomet was fucceeded by Ochali, a renegado, who reduced the kingdom of Tunis. It remained fubject to the viceroy of Algiers only till the year 1586, when a bafhaw of Tunis was appointed by the Sultan.

Algiers continued to be governed, till the beginning of the feventeenth century, by Turkifh viceroys or bafhaws. At laft, the Turkifh Janifaries and militia becoming powerful enough to fupprefs the tyrannic fway of thofe bafhaws, they fent a deputation of fome of their chief members to Conftantinople to complain of their rapacity. They reprefented to the miniftry, how much more honourable it would be for the grand feignior to permit them to chufe their own dey, or governor, from among themfelves, whofe intereft it would be to fee that the revenue of the country was rightly applied in keeping up its forces complete, and in fupplying all other exigencies of the ftate, without any farther charge or trouble to the porte, than that of allowing them its protection. Algiers was to be wholly left under the direction of the dey and his divan. The power of the Turkifh bafhaw was to be reduced to a fhadow.

Thefe propofals were accepted by the porte. The divan elected a dey from among themfelves.. They compiled a new fet of laws and made feveral regulations for the better fupport and maintenance of this new form of government. The fubfequent altercations that frequently happened between the bafhaws and deys, the one endeavouring to recover their former power, and the other to curtail it, caufed fuch frequent complaints and difcontents at the Ottoman court, as made them fometimes repent of their compliance.

In the year 1601, the Spaniards made another attempt upon Algiers. Their fleet was driven back by contrary winds, fo that they came off without lofs. In 1609, the Moors being expelled from Spain, flocked in great numbers to Algiers; and as many of them were very able failors, they undoubtedly contributed to make the Algerine fleet fo formidable as it became foon after. In 1616, their fleet confifted of forty fhips between two hundred and four hundred tons burthen, and their admiral was five hundred tons. It was divided into two fquadrons, one of eighteen fail, ftationed before the port of Malaga; and the other at the Cape of Santa Maria, between Lifbon and Seville; both of which attacked Chriftian fhips, both Englifh and French, with whom they pretended to be in friendfhip, as well as Spaniards, and Portuguefe, with whom they were at war.

The Algerines were now become formidable to the European powers. The Spaniards, who were moft in danger, folicited the affiftance of England, the Pope, and other ftates. The French, however, were the firft who dared to fhew their refentment at the perfidious

behaviour of thefe mifcreants; and in 1617, M. Beau-
lieu was fent againft them with a fleet of fifty men of
war. He defeated their fleet, and took two of their
veffels. Their admiral funk his own fhip and crew,
rather than fall into the hands of the enemy.

In 1620, a fquadron of Englifh men of war was fent
againft Algiers, but did nothing. The Algerines, becoming more infolent, openly defied all the European
powers, the Dutch only excepted, to whom, in 1625,
they fent a propofal, that in cafe they would fit out
twenty fail of fhips in the following year, upon any
fervice againft the Spaniards, the corfairs would join
them with fixty fail.

Next year; the Cologlies, or children of fuch Turks
as had been permitted to marry at Algiers, who were
inrolled in the militia, feized on the citadel, and had
well nigh made themfelves mafters of the city. They
were attacked by the Turks and renegadoes, who
defeated them with terrible flaughter. Numbers
were executed, and their heads thrown in heaps on the
city walls.

In 1623, the Algerines and other ftates of Barbary,
threw off their dependence on the porte. Sultan Amu-
rath IV. had been obliged to make a truce for twenty five
years, with the emperor Ferdinand II. As this put a ftop to
the piratical trade of the Algerines, they proceeded as
above mentioned ; and refolved, that whoever defired
to be at peace with them, muft, feparately, apply to their
own government. They began to make prizes of feveral merchant fhips belonging to the powers at peace
with the porte. They feized a Dutch fhip and poleacre
at Scanderoon ; they even ventured on fhore, and finding the town abandoned by the Turkifh aga and inhabitants, they plundered all the magazines and ware-hou-
fes, and fet them on fire. About this time, Louis XIII.
undertook to build a fort on their coafts, inftead of one
formerly built by the Marfilians, and which had been
demolifhed. This, after fome difficulty, he accomplifhed;
and it was called the Baftion of France, but the fituation being found inconvenient, the French purchafed
the port of La Calle, and obtained liberty to trade with

the Arabians and Moors. The Ottoman court, in the mean time, was so much embarrassed with a Persian war, that there was no leisure to check the Algerines piracies. This gave an opportunity to the vizir and other courtiers to compound matters with the Algerines, and to get a share of the prizes, which were very considerable. For the sake of form a severe reprimand, accompanied with threats, was sent them. They replied, that " they deserved to be indulged in these depredati-
" ons, as they were the only bulwark against the Chris-
" tian powers, and in particular, against the Spaniards,
" the sworn enemies of the Moslem name." They added, that " if they should pay a punctilious regard to
" all who could purchase liberty to trade with the Ot-
" toman empire, they would have nothing to do but
" set fire to their shipping, and turn camel-drivers."

In the year 1635, four brothers of a family in France, entered into an undertaking so desperate, that perhaps the annals of knight-errantry can scarcely furnish its equal. This was no less than to retort the piracies of the Algerines, upon themselves; and as they indiscriminately took the ships of all nations, so were these heroes indiscriminately to take the ships belonging to Algiers; and this with a small frigate of ten guns! An hundred volunteers embarked; a Maltese commission was obtained, with an able master, and thirty mariners. On their first setting out, they took, on the Spanish coast, a ship laden with wine. Three days after, they engaged two large Algerine corsairs, one of twenty and the other of twenty-four guns. The French made so desperate a resistance, that the pirates were not able to take them, till five other corsairs came up. The French vessel, being almost torn to pieces, was then boarded and taken. In 1642, the brothers redeemed themselves, at the price of six thousand dollars.

In 1637, the Algerines infested the British channel; and, according to Mrs Macauley, * had made such a vast number of captures, as to have at one time, between four and five thousand subjects of England prisoners.

* History of England vol. II. chap. 4.

The Algerines profecuted their piracies with impunity, to the terror and difgrace of Chriftendom, till the year 1652; when a French fleet being accidentally driven to Algiers, the admiral took it into his head to demand a releafe of all the captives of his nation without exception. This being refufed, the Frenchman without ceremony carried off the Turkifh viceroy, and his cadi or judge, who were juft arrived from the porte, with all their equipage and retinue. The Algerines, by way of reprifal, furprifed the Baftion of France already mentioned, and carried off the inhabitants to the number of fix hundred, with all their effects. Upon this, the admiral fent them word, that he would pay them another vifit, next year, with his whole fleet.

The Algerines fitted out a fleet of fixteen galleys and galliots, under the command of Hali Pinchinin. The chief defign of this armament was againft the treafure of Loretto; which they were prevented by contrary winds from obtaining. Hereupon they made a defcent on Puglia in the kingdom of Naples; where they ravaged the whole territory of Necotra. They carried off a vaft number of captives. Thence fteering towards Dalmatia, they fcoured the Adriatic, and loaded themfelves with immenfe plunder.

The Venetians, alarmed at fuch ravages, equipped a fleet of twenty-eight fail, under the command of admiral Capello, with exprefs orders to burn, fink, or take, all the Barbary corfairs which he met with, either on the open feas, or even in the Ottoman harbours, agreeable to a late treaty of peace with the porte. On the other hand, the captain bafhaw, who had been fent out with a Turkifh fleet to chace the Florentine and Maltefe cruifers from the Archipelago, learning that the Algerine fquadron was fo near, fent exprefs orders to the admiral to come to his affiftance. Pinchinin readily agreed; but he was overtaken by Capello, from whom he retired to Valona, a fea-port belonging to the grand feignior, whither the Venetian admiral purfued him; but the Turkifh governor refufing to turn out the pirates, according to the articles of the peace between the Ottoman court and Venice, Capello was obliged to con-

tent himfelf with watching them for fome time. Pinchinin foon ventured out, an engagement immediately en-
fued, and the Algerines were defeated. Five of the rveffels
were difabled; one thoufand five hundred men, Turks,
and Chriftian flaves, were killed; befides one thoufand
fix hundred galley flaves who regained their liberty.
Pinchinin, after this defeat, returned to Valona, where
he was again watched by Capello, but the latter had not
lain long at his old anchorage, before he received a letter from the fenate, defiring him to make no farther
attempt on the pirates at that time, for fear of a rupture
with the porte. Capello was forced to fubmit; but
refolving to take fuch a leave of the Algerines as he
thought they deferved, obferved how they had reared
their tents, and drawn their booty and equipage along
the fhore. He then kept firing among their tents, while
fome well manned galliots and brigantines were difpatched to attack their fhipping. Sixteen gallies, with
all their cannon, and ftores, were towed out. In this
laft engagement, a ball from one of the Venetian gallies, ftruck a Turkifh mofque, and hence, the whole action was confidered as an infult to the grand feignior.
To conceal this, Capello was ordered to fink all the Algerine fhips that he had taken, except the admiral;
which was to be conducted to Venice, and laid up as a
trophy. Capello received a fevere reprimand, and the
Venetians were obliged to buy, with five hundred thoufand ducats, a peace from the porte.

In the mean time, the news of this defeat and lofs
filled Algiers with rage and confufion. The city was
on the point of an infurrection, when the bafhaw pub-
lifhed a proclamation, forbidding, not only complaints
and outcries, under the fevereft penalties, but all perfons whatever to take their thumbs from within their
girdles, while they were deliberating on this fubject.
They applied to the porte for an order, that the Venetians
fettled in the Levant, fhould make up their lofs. But
with this the grand feignior refufed to comply, and left
them to repair their loffes, and to build new fhips in the
beft manner that they could. It was not long, however,
before they had the fatisfaction of feeing one of their

and, with a frefh fupply of fix hundred flaves, whom he had brought from the coaft of Iceland, whither he had been directed by a mifcreant native taken on board a Danifh fhip.

CHAPTER IV.

Pinchinin. His engagement with a Dutch fhip. Bombardment and Deftruction of Algiers, by the French. Defeat of the Spaniards.

THE pirates did not long continue in their weak and defencelefs ftate; being able, at the end of two years, to appear at fea with a fleet of fixty five fail. The Admiral Pinchinin equipped four galliots at his own expence; with which, in conjunction with the Chiayah or fecretary of the bafhaw of Tripoli, he made a fecond excurfion. This fmall fquadron, confifting of five galleys and two brigantines, fell in with an Englifh fhip of forty guns; which, however, Pinchinin's captains refufed to engage, but being afterwards reproached by him for their cowardice, they fwore to attack the next Chriftian fhip that came in their way. This happened to be a Dutch merchantman, of twenty eight guns and forty men, deeply laden, and difabled by a calm from ufing her fails. Pinchinin immediately fummoned her to furrender; but receiving an ironical anfwer, drew up his fquadron in form of an half moon, that they might pour their fhot all at once into their adverfary. This, however, the Dutchman avoided, by means of a breeze of wind which fortunately fprung up and enabled him to turn his fhip; by which the galleys ran foul of each other. Upon this Pinchinin ran his own galley along fide the merchantman, the upper deck of which feventy Algerines immediately took poffeffion of, fome of them cutting the rigging, others plying the hatches with hand-grenadoes; but the Dutch having fecured themfelves in their clofe quarters, began to fire at the Algerines on board, from two pieces of cannon loaded with fmall fhot; by which they were all foon killed or forced to fubmit. Pinchinin, in the mean time, made feveral unfuccefsful attempts to relieve his men, as well as to furround the Dutch with his other galleys; but their fhip lay fo deep in the water, that every fhot did terrible execution among the pirates; fo that they were obliged to remove farther off. At laft the Dutch captain, having ordered his guns to be loaded with cartouches, gave them a parting volley which killed, as it is faid, two hundred of them, and fent the reft back to Algiers in a difmal condition.

But though Pinchinin thus returned in difgrace, the reft of the fleet quickly came back with vaft numbers of flaves, and an immenfe quantity of rich fpoils; in fo much that the Englifh, French, and Dutch, were obliged to cringe to the Algerines, who fometimes condefcended to be at peace with them, but fwore eternal war againft Spain, Portugal, and Italy, whom they confidered as the greateft enemies to the Mahometan name. At laft Lewis the fourteenth, provoked by the grievous outrages committed by the Algerines on the coafts of Provence and Languedoc, ordered, in 1681, a confiderable fleet to be fitted out againft them, under the Marquis du Quefne, vice admiral of France. His firft expedition was againft a number of Tripolitan corfairs; who had the good fortune to outrow him, and fhelter themfelves iu the ifland of Scio belonging to the Turks. This did not prevent him from purfuing them thither, and making fuch a terrible fire upon them, as deftroyed fourteen of their veffels, befides battering the walls of the caftle.

This feverity feemed only to be defigned as a check to the piracies of the Algerines; but, finding that they ftill continued their outrages on the French coaft, Du Quefne failed in Auguft, 1682, to Algiers, cannonading and bombarding it fo furioufly, that, in a very fhort time, the whole town was in flames. The great mofque was battered down, and moft of the houfes laid in ruins, fo that the inhabitants were on the point of abandoning the place; when, on a fudden, the wind turned about, and obliged Du Quefne to return to Toulon. The Algerines immediately made reprifals,

By fending a number of galleys and galliots to the coafts of Provence, where they committed the most dreadful ravages, and brought away a vaft number of captives; upon which a new armament was ordered to be got ready at Toulon and Marfeilles, againft them the next year; and the Algerines, having received early notice, put themfelves into as good a ftate of defence as the time would allow.

In May, 1683, Du Quefne with his fquadron caft anchor before Algiers; where, being joined by the marquis d'Affranville, at the head of five ftrong vefTels, it was refolved to bombard the town next day, when accordingly, one hundred bombs were thrown into it which did terrible execution, while the befieged made fome hundred difcharges of their cannon againft the affailants, without doing any confiderable damage. The following night, bombs were again thrown into the city in fuch numbers, that the dey's palace and other great edifices were almoft deftroyed; fome of the batteries were difmounted, and feveral vefTels funk in the port. The dey, and Turkifh bafhaw, as well as the whole foldiery, alarmed at this dreadful havock, immedily fued for peace. As a preliminary, the French infifted on the furrender of all Chriftian captives who had been taken fighting under their flag, which being granted, one hundred and forty two perfons were directly delivered up, with a promife of fending on board the remainder, as foon as they could be got from the different parts of the country. Accordingly Du Quefne fent his commifTary-general and one of his engineers into the town; but with exprefs orders to infift upon the delivery of all the French captives without excepception, together with the effects that had been taken from the French; and that Mezomorto their then admiral, and Hali Rais one of their captains, fhould be given as hoftages.

This laft demand having embarrafTed the dey, he afTembled the divan, and acquainted them with it. Upon this Mezomorto fell into a violent pafTion, and told the afTembly, that the cowardice of thofe who fat at the helm had occafioned the ruin of Algiers; but, that for his part, he would never confent to deliver up any thing that was taken from the French. He immadietely acquainted the foldiery with what had paffed; which fo exafperated them, that they murdered the dey that very night, and on the morrow chofe Mezomorto in his place. This was no fooner done, than he cancelled all the articles of peace which had been made, and hoftilities were renewed with greater fury than ever.

The French admiral now kept pouring in fuch volleys of bombs, that in lefs than three days, the greateft part of the city was reduced to afhes; and the fire burnt with fuch fury, that the fea was enlightened for more than two leagues round. Mezomorto, unmoved by all thefe difafters, and the vaft numbers of the flain, whofe blood ran in rivulets along the ftreets; or rather, grown furious and defperate, fought only how to wreak his revenge on the enemy; and, not content with caufing all the French in the city to be cruelly murdered, he ordered their conful to be tied hand and foot, and faftened alive to the mouth of a mortar, from which he was fhot away againft their navy. By this piece of inhumanity, Du Quefne was fo exafperated, that he did did not leave Algiers till he had utterly deftroyed all their fortifications, fhipping, almoft all the lower part, and above two thirds of the upper part of the city; which became little more than an heap of ruins.

The Algerines were now thoroughly convinced that they were not invincible; and, therefore, immediately fent an embaffy into France, begging in the moft abject terms for peace; which Lewis very foon granted, to their inexpreffible joy. They now began to pay fome regard to other nations, and to be fomewhat cautious how they wantonly provoked their difpleafure. The firft bombardment by the French had fo far humbled the Algerines, that they condefcended to enter into a treaty with England; which was in 1686 renewed upon terms very advantageous to the latter. tI is not to be fuppofed, however, that the natural perfidy of the Algerines would difappear on a fudden. Notwithftanding this treaty, therefore, they loft no opportunity of making prizes of Englifh fhips, when they could conveniently feize them. Upon fome infringement of this kind, captain Beach, in 1695, drove afhore and burned feven of their frigates which produced a renewal of the treaty five years after; but it was not until the taking of Gibraltar and Port Mahon, that Britain could have a fufficient check upon them to enforce the obfervation of treaties; and thefe have fince proved fuch reftraints upon Algiers, that they ftill continue to pay a greater deference to the Englifh than to any other European power.

In 1708, Oran, as has been already related, was taken by the Algerines from the Spaniards, and recovered by the latter in 1732. The Turkifh bafhaw was in 1710, finally expelled.

Since the laft fiege of Oran the moft remarkable event in the annals of Barbary is the attack of Algiers, by the Spaniards in the year 1775. With a concife account of that expedition, we fhall clofe this chapter of blood.

On the 23d of June 1775, a fleet of fix fhips of the line, twelve frigates and thirty three other armed veffels fet fail from Carthagena, in Spain, to attack Algiers. There was on board a body of troops amounting to twenty four thoufand four hundred and forty feven men, including infantry, cavalry, marines, and fix hundred deferters deftined to ferve as workmen. They were commanded by the count O'Reilly, a perfonal favourite of the late king of Spain. They had likewife for the land fervice, an hundred and feventy-fix pieces of artillery, mortars, and howitzers, with a fuitable quantity of military ftores. On the 30th of June, and 1ft of July, they anchored in the bay of Algiers. They obferved a large encampment, placed behind a battery, eaft of the river Xarach, which runs on the eaftward of the city. On the 2d of July, a council was held; and orders were given that the troops fhould hold themfelves in readinefs to difembark next morning, by day break. But as the fucceeding night was windy, and a fwell had fet in from the fhore, thefe orders were countermanded. From this day, to the 6th, there were frequent councils, violent debates, and nothing done. A quarrel broke out between O'Reilly and the Marquis de Romana, a Spanish major-general, who was killed in the subsequent action. On the 6th, the principal officers were again assembled, to receive their ultimate instructions. The commander in chief warned the army, that it was the custom of the Moors, to pretend a most violent attack, and on the smallest resistance, to fly with precipitation, that they might draw the enemy into an ambuscade. He cautioned the troops not to break their ranks, as nothing but the force of discipline could secure them against so active an enemy. He pointed out the very error which they soon after committed, and the snare into which they were betrayed. On landing, the army was directed to gain some heights, which were supposed requisite to ensure success against Algiers. In the afternoon of the 6th, some ships of war were ordered to fire against three batteries to the eastward of that city. This commission was executed with so much laudable attention to the personal safety of the assailants, if such we may term them, that their shot *did not reach the shore*, those of one seventy-four gun ship excepted. At sun-set this formidable attack ceased.

On the 7th at day-break, between eight and nine thousand men were put on board the boats for landing. They advanced, under the protection of some larger vessels very near the coast. Not a Moor appeared to oppose them; and at seven o'clock in the morning, they *returned on board the transports*. Not a shot was fired on either side, during the whole day.

On the 8th, at day-break, the ships being stationed to batter the different forts to the right and left of the place of disembarkation, the troops, to the number of about eight thousand, were put on board the boats; which formed in six columns. The place of landing was a league and an half to the eastward of the city of Algiers. Eighty thousand Moors, of whom two thirds were cavalry, came in sight, but did not attempt to oppose the landing of the Spanish forces. It is said, that the whole number of Africans collected on this occafion, was not lefs than one hundred and fifty thoufand, The troops advanced into a clofe country, which the Algerines had occupied in fmall parties. . The grenadiers and light infantry of the Spaniards were repulfed, and the whole body fell into confufion. In a very fhort time they fled, leaving behind them a great number of killed and wounded. The latter, a few excepted, were, in fpite of their intreaties, left to the *mercy* of the conquerors. Part of a fecond embarkation of troops added to the general confufion. A third body had caft up an entrenchment on the fhore, for the protection of the army. The Africans attacked it, but were driven back with great flaughter on both fides. The Spaniards, in their gazette, acknowledged the lofs of five hundred and twenty one men killed, and two thoufand two hundred and feventy nine wounded. It is faid, that the Algerines had between five and fix thoufand men flain on the fpot. The wounded Spaniards, who were left on the field of battle, were every one murdered by the enemy. The government of Algiers had offered ten zequins for the head of each Spaniard. Fifteen pieces of cannon, and three howitzers were left behind by thefe unfortunate invaders. The real amount of their lofs can hardly have been lefs than three thoufand lives, and was perhaps confiderably greater. In the gazette of a court, we feldom expect an honeft reckoning of this kind. If the writer of that of Madrid intended us to believe that two thoufand two hundred and feventy-nine of the wounded were brought off, the officer from whofe journal this account is extracted, fays that a much greater number were left behind, than were faved, which makes the ftory worfe and worfe. On details of this kind, we cannot dwell with pleafure. One circumftance is evident, that the Spanifh commanders did not underftand their bufinefs.*

---

* This narrative is extracted from a journal printed by major William Dalrymple, at the end of his Travels through Spain and Portugal, printed at London, in 1777. The trite tale of a dey of Algiers having offered to burn the city for fifty thoufand pounds, is a defpicable newspaper fiction.

CHAPTER V.

State of America as to Algiers. Conduct of Britain. Concluding Remarks.

IN the two laſt Chapters, we have ſeen the Algerines ſucceſſively ſet at defiance, ſeveral of the moſt formidable nations of Europe. When the United States of America had obtained their infant independence, it was naturally to be expeĉted, that they alſo ſhould, in ſome degree, ſuffer, by the ravages of the corſairs. Various circumſtances pointed them out, as eligible objeĉts of piratical rapine. They poſſeſſed an extenſive trade with Europe, which in the firſt place, preſented a ſplended temptation to plunder. There was, on the part of the Algerines, a ſecond and irreſiſtible motive to hoſtilities. America did not ſupport, at her national expence, any maritime force whatever; and thirdly, had ſhe even eſtabliſhed an armed navy, this country lies at the diſtance of more than three thouſand miles, from the common range of the privateers of Barbary. Hence, to reduce them to ſubmiſſion, muſt always require a proportion of trouble and expence greatly ſuperior to the ſubſtantial magnitude of the objeĉt of attack; and this remoteneſs of our ſituation might be conſidered as an additional inducement to the regency of Algiers for interrupting our navigation. Of the number and ſtrength of the corſairs, it is impoſſible to give an accurate ſtatement. Their aĉtual force, however, compared, with that which the United States could eaſily fit out, is but trifling. To bring their whole ſhips of war, at once, to a regular engagement, never can be praĉticable, but ſhould it happen, it may without preſumption be ſuppoſed, that fifteen or twenty American forty gun frigates would ſend heir navy to the bottom. When we refleĉt on the numerous and peculiar incitements which theſe Africans had, to commence depredations on the commerce of the United States, inſtead of being ſurpriſed at our having ſuffered ſo much, it rather becomes an objeĉt of wonder that we have fuffered fo little. The late alarming intelligence from Lifbon has excited univer-fal attention from the public to that fubject, which may be divided into two queftions. Firft, why, excepting two veffels,* have not the fhips of this country met with any interruption fince the end of the war with Britain? Second, why has our trade now fuffered fo unexpected and fevere a check?

In anfwer to the firft query, it has happened, that fince the independence of North-America, the Algerines have been conftantly at war, with the Dutch, or the Portuguefe, or both at once; and as either of thefe na-tions is greatly fuperior, in regular ftrength at fea, to the corfairs, they have, hitherto, for the fecurity of their own commerce, watched the entrance of the Mediter-ranean fo carefully, that the corfairs have been feldom able to get out of it. That they fometimes did fo is unfortunately certain, from the fate of the two Ameri-can veffels above-mentioned; but, in general, they were fhut up in the Mediterranean, as in a prifon, without a poffibility of extending their depredations on the At-lantic ocean. Into the former, American veffels but fometimes ventured, and when they did fo, they derived fecurity from forged or purchafed Mediterranean paffes. A Britifh fhip has for her protection a pafs, which is written on a large fheet of parchment, and has, by way of ornament, fome figures or dafhes drawn with a pen, or engraved on the margin. The Algerines cannot read Englifh, and it would moft likely coft the captain

* On the 25th of July, 1785, the fchooner Maria, captain Stephens, belonging to Mr. Forfter, of Bofton, was taken off Cape St. Vincents, by an Algerine cruifer; and five days after-wards, the fhip Dolphin, captain O'Brien, belonging to Meffrs Irvines of Philadelphia, was taken by another, fifty leagues weftward of Lisbon. Thefe veffels, with their cargoes, and crews, twenty one in number, were carried into Algiers. Of this number two have been ranfomed by their friends. The remainder now reduced by death to thirteen, are yet flaves. In the newfpa-pers about that time, two or three other fhips are reported as captured, but upon enquiry, thefe two veffels only appear to have been fo.

of a corfair his head, were he to carry a Britifh veffel, by miftake, as a prize into the harbour of Algiers. They have adopted a *sagacious* contrivance to difcover whether fuch paffes are genuine. They keep a ftick marked with notches correfponding to the fhape of thofe figures, that are uniformly delineated on the margin of the parchment. When the pafs is produced, their mea- fure is applied. In this way, it cannot be difficult for the moft bungling artift, who has an original pafs before him, to deceive them, and, by this means, it is faid, upon reputable authority, that many veffels have been preferved. Befides, even in the Mediterranean itfelf, the progrefs of the Algerines has been confiderably cramped by the Portuguefe and Dutch fhips of war, and both thefe nations, as well as the Spaniards, from a regard to their own intereft, as well as from the com- mon principles of juftice and humanity, have been for- ward to extend their protection to the American flag.

In anfwer to the fecond query, this protection has, at prefent been fufpended, becaufe a ceffation of hoftili- ties has taken place between Holland and Portugal on the one fide, and the regency of Algiers on the other. Spain, at the fame time, has been engaged in the gene- ral confpiracy of the Domitians and Caligulas of Eu- rope, againft the republic of France; and as this coun- try has contracted the guilt of becoming a free nation, we likewife are involved, though, *as yet*, but at fecond hand, in the vengeance of the imperial and royal Van- dals. The corfairs of Barbary are now at liberty to attack the veffels of the United States, not only in the Mediterranean, but alfo in the Atlantic ocean. From the final eftablifhment of American independence, fome attempts are reported to have been made by the American government, to conclude a pacification with the ftate of Algiers, but for fome reafon or other, thefe attempts have hitherto proved unfuccefsful. The circumftances which have always difappointed the pa- cific defigns of our adminiftration, deferve to be invef- tigated; but before we proceed to that fubject, it may not be improper to ftate in a few words the fituation of this country, with refpect to the emperor of Morocco,

A treaty of peace and commerce between that prince, and America, having been concluded by the agency of Mr. Thomas Barclay, was ratified by Congrefs at New-York, on the 18th of July, 1787. It confifts of twenty five articles. Want of room prevents its infertion entire in this place, but the third and fifth claufes merit at this juncture, the moft particular attention; and are in thefe words.

Art. III. *If either of the parties fhall be at war with any nation whatever, and take a prize belonging to that nation, and there fhall be found on board fubjects or effects belonging to either of the parties, the fubjects fhall be fet at liberty, and* the effects returned to the owners. *And if any goods, belonging to any nation, with whom either of the parties fhall be at war, fhall be loaded in veffels belonging to the other party,* they fhall pafs free and unmolefted, without any attempt being made to take or detain them.

Art. V. *If either of the parties fhall be at war, and meet a veffel at fea belonging to the other, it is agreed that if an examination is to be made, it fhall be done* by fending a boat with two or three men only, *and if any gun fhall be fired, and injury done without reafon, the offending party fhall make good all damages.*

The twenty-fifth, and laft article is in thefe words : *This treaty fhall continue in full force, with the help of God, for fifty years.* A moft defirable event.

Let us compare the tenor of this treaty, which remains unviolated, with the prefent conduct of Britain, of Ruffia, and of Spain, towards the United States of America. We fhall then be convinced, that in a contraft with the fovereigns of thefe three nations, the emperor of Morocco is a monarch of juftice and humanity.

Several of our late letters from Lifbon agree in afferting, that the prefent peace or truce between Algiers and Portugal has been formed by the officious intervention of England, without the knowledge of the latter. The fame advices add, and their information is univerfally believed, that this has been done by England, that the corfairs of Barbary might have liberty to interrupt the commerce of this country with Europe.

Since the commencement of the unfortunate war, that now spreads desolation and bankruptcy over so many countries, in that quarter of the world, American bottoms, because they were neutral, obtained the preference to those of England in the carrying trade. *They were not liable to be seized by French privateers,* and could, therefore, unmolested, transport the commodities of any one country to any other. This advantage gave our vessels a decided superiority; and the master of an American ship frequently received twenty per cent. more for the same freight, than would be given to the master of an English vessel. This humiliating distinction alarmed the pride of the English nation. Divested of the carrying trade, the naval despotism of England would at once shrink into nothing. The powers of Europe may reduce her to the natural level of her importance, without the expense of firing a single gun. Let them declare, that no vessel of that country shall bring into their harbours, any commodities but those of British growth or manufacture. Her navy, which has perpetrated such incessant mischief, would then, if I may borrow the trite quotation from Shakespeare, vanish, *like the baseless fabric of a vision.*

The Americans, for some time past, have been making rapid strides towards her expulsion from the carrying trade. England could hardly venture, at this crisis, to add a second republic to the catalogue of her enemies. She has, therefore, adopted the miserable expedient of turning loose the Algerines, that these execrable ruffians might plunder our property, and plunge our fellow-citizens into slavery.

Lord Sheffield, in a pamphlet which has obtained more notice than it deserved, informs the English nation, " That it will not be the interest of any of the " great maritime powers, to protect the American ves- " sels from the Barbary states." This benevolent remark has received a proper answer from the author of " Observations" on his lordship's pamphlet. The moderation of stile, the candour of reasoning, and the unquestioned authenticity of the facts advanced by Mr. Coxe, deserve, in an uncommon degree, the attention, and the gratitude of his countrymen,

The public have juſt been informed of a reſolution paſſed by Congreſs. A naval force is to be fitted out adequate to the protection of our commerce againſt the Algerines ; or to ſpeak with propriety, againſt the *African emiſſaries of England.* It is not impoſſible that the buſineſs will end by a trip to the Bahama iſlands. They contain a gang of pirates, who deſerve a gibbet ſtill better than the diſciples of Barbaroſſa.

The following lines are extracted from a " Poem on the happineſs of America," by colonel Humphrey . We cannot agree with this writer, that Britain is the " Firſt of nations, and " the queen of iſles ;" or that the Algerines are the " feebleſt" of men. Yet, upon the whole, theſe verſes are ſpirited and poetical.

HOW long will heav'n reſtrain its burſting ire,
Nor rain blue tempeſts of devouring fire?
How long ſhall widows weep their ſons in vain,
The prop of years in ſlav'ry's iron chain?
How long the love-ſick maid, unheeded, rove
The ſounding ſhore, and call her abſent love ;
With waſting tears and ſighs his lot bewail,
And ſeem to ſee him in each coming ſail ?
How long the merchant turn his failing eyes,
In deſperation, on the ſeas and ſkies,
And aſk his captur'd ſhips, his raviſh'd goods,
With frantic ravings, of the heav'ns and floods?
  How long, Columbians dear ! will ye complain
Of theſe curſt inſults on the open main ?
In timid ſloth, ſhall injur'd brav'ry ſleep?
Awake ! awake ! avengers of the deep !
Revenge ! revenge ! the voice of nature cries;
Awake to glory, and to vengeance riſe !
To arms ! to arms ! ye bold indignant bands!
'Tis heav'n inſpires ; 'tis God himſelf commands
Save human nature from ſuch deadly harms,
By force of reaſon, or by force of arms.
  O ye great powers, who paſſports baſely crave,
From Afric's lords to ſail the midland wave—
Great fallen pow'rs, whoſe gems and golden bribes
Buy paltry paſſports from theſe ſavage tribes—
Ye, whoſe fine purples, ſilks, and ſtuffs of gold
(An annual tribute) their dark limbs infold—

Ye, whofe mean policy for them equips,
To plague mankind, the predatory fhips—
Why will you buy your infamy fo dear ?
Is it felf-int'reft, or a daftard fear ?
Is it becaufe ye meanly think to gain
A richer commerce on th' infefted main ?
Is it becaufe ye meanly wifh to fee
Your rivals chain'd, yourfelves ignobly free ?
Who gave commiffions to thefe monfters fierce,
To hold in chains the humbled univerfe ?
Would God, would nature, wou'd their conqu'ring fwords,
Without your meannefs, make them ocean's lords ?
What ! Do you fear ? nor dare their power provoke?
Would not that bubble burft beneath your ftroke ?
And fhall the weak remains of barb'rous rage,
Infulting, triumph o'er th' enlighten'd age ?
Do ye not feel confufion, horror, fhame,
To bear a hateful, tributary name ?
Will ye not aid to wipe the foul difgrace,
And break the fetters from the human race ?
   Then, though unaided by thofe mighty powers,
Ours be the toil ; the danger, glory ours :
Then, O my friends, by heav'n ordain'd to free,
From tyrant rage, the long infefted fea—
Then let us firm, though folitary, ftand,
The fword, and olive branch in either hand :
An equal peace propofe with reafon's voice,
Or rufh to arms, if arms fhould be their choice.
   Stung by their crimes, can aught your vengeance ftay ?
Can terror daunt you ? or can death difmay ?
The foul enrag'd, can threats, can tortures tame,
Or the dark dungeon quench th'etherial flame ?
Have ye not once to heav'n's dread throne appeal'd,
And has not heav'n your independence feal'd ?
What was the power ye dar'd that time engage,
And brave the terrors of its hoftile rage ?
Was it not Britain, great in warlike toils,
The firft of nations, as the queen of ifles—
Britain, whofe fleets, that rul'd the briny furge,
Made navies tremble to its utmoft verge,
Whofe fingle arm held half the world at odds,
Great nurfe of fages, bards, and demigods !
But what are thefe whofe threat'nings round you burft!
Of men the dregs, the feebleft, vileft, worft ;
Thefe are the pirates from the Barb'ry ftrand,
Audacious mifcreants, fierce, yet feeble band !
Who, impious, dare (no provocation giv'n)
Infult the rights of man—the laws of heav'n !

www.ingramcontent.com/pod-product-compliance
Lightning Source LLC
Chambersburg PA
CBHW021546270326
41930CB00008B/1375

* 9 7 8 3 7 4 3 3 6 8 7 4 3 *